Design: Judith Chant and Alison Lee
Recipe Photography: Peter Barry
Jacket and Illustration Artwork: Jane Winton, courtesy of
Bernard Thornton Artists, London
Editor: Josephine Bacon

CHARTWELL BOOKS
a division of Book Sales, Inc.
POST OFFICE BOX 7100
114 Northfield Avenue
Edison, NJ 08818-7100

CLB 4261
© 1995 CLB Publishing, Godalming, Surrey, U.K.
All rights reserved
Printed and bound in Singapore
ISBN 0-7858-0291-6

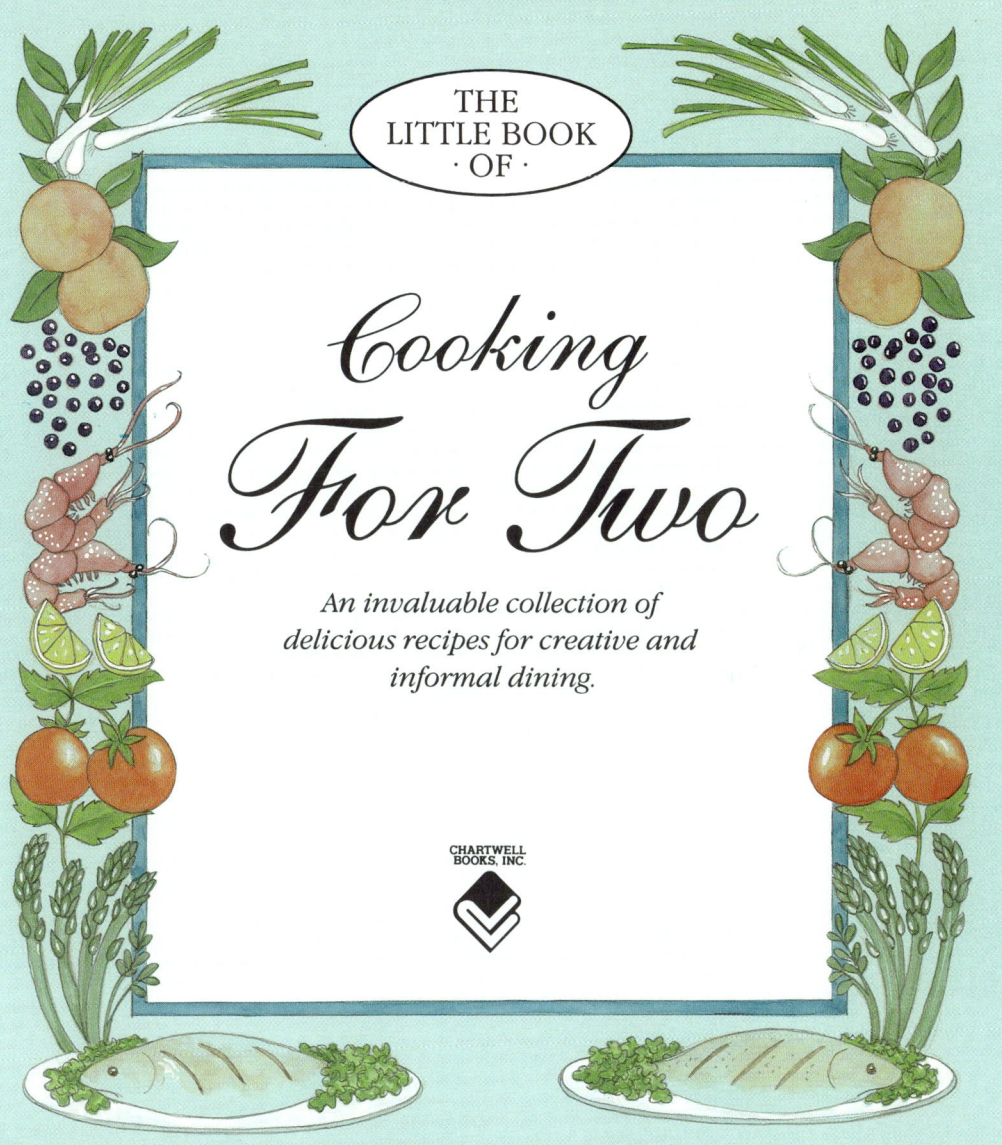

THE LITTLE BOOK ·OF·

Cooking For Two

An invaluable collection of delicious recipes for creative and informal dining.

CHARTWELL BOOKS, INC.

Introduction

Choosing just what to cook when there are only two of you to cook for can be a hard task. Something requiring a great deal of care and attention often does not seem worthwhile, or quite likely you just do not have the time. For many people, a lack of time means turning to TV dinners rather than actually preparing something themselves. This situation, though understandable, is far from ideal. The majority of convenience meals are expensive, not always healthy, and leave a lot to be desired in terms of taste.

The secret to preparing meals for two is to incorporate an unusual ingredient, something a little out of the ordinary in the form of, say, herbs, spices, and dried fruit and nuts, all of which can be conveniently kept in the store cupboard ready for use.

When cooking for two, the best dishes to choose for everyday meals, particularly if you are starting after a day's work, are those that are quick and easy to prepare – the more lengthy ones can always be saved for the weekend. Rice, pasta and salads make good accompaniments for convenient mid-week meals. If meat is on the menu, the most appropriate cuts are quick cooking ones such as steaks, chops and scallops. Chicken is particularly good as it quick and easy to cook and available in so many different

cuts. Fish is also an ideal buy, as it is available ready-prepared and is both quick-cooking and healthy.

There are some aspects of our high-tech modern world that actually make it far easier to shop and cook for two than ever before. Self-service weighing scales in the stores enable the shopper to buy small amounts, such as two or three items of fruit, or a single head of broccoli, a few chilies, or whatever, without incurring the storekeeper's wrath. Also, once home with the shopping, the microwave can be of tremendous help, particularly when cooking vegetables and reheating precooked dishes. Of course, the freezer, too, has obvious advantages when dealing with small quantities. Large quantities of delicious dishes can be made, divided into portions and frozen for later use. This allows you to maximise your time with the minimum of effort.

The cook dealing with small amounts generally does not want to spend too long preparing complex meals, but he or she is likely to want to make something enjoyable to linger over, especially if cooking for a partner, and that is what this book is all about. Armed with this collection of rather special recipes, cooking for two will become a real pleasure.

Fried Squid

SERVES 2

Serve this sweet and delicious seafood as a appetizer. It's easier to prepare than you think!

PREPARATION: 20 mins
COOKING: 3 mins per batch

3 cups small, fresh squid
2 tbsps all-purpose flour
Salt and pepper
Oil for deep-frying
Lemon wedges and parsley for garnishing

1. Hold the body of the squid with one hand and the head with the other and pull gently to separate. Remove the intestines and the quill, which is clear and plastic-like. Rinse the body of the squid inside and outside under cold running water.

2. Cut the tentacles from the head, just above

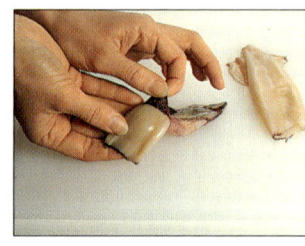

Step 3 Remove the outer skin from the body of the squid and cut the body into thin rings.

Step 2 Cut the tentacles from the head just above the eye and separate them into individual pieces.

the eye. Separate into individual tentacles.

3. Remove the brownish or purplish outer skin from the body of the squid and cut the flesh into ¼-inch rings.

4. Mix the flour, salt, and pepper together on a sheet of paper or in a shallow dish. Toss the rings of squid and the tentacles in the flour mixture to coat. Heat the oil to 350°F in a large skillet and fry the squid, about 6 pieces at a time, saving the tentacles until last. Cook about 3 minutes or until lightly browned and crisp. Remove them from the oil with a slotted spoon and drain on kitchen paper. Sprinkle lightly with salt and continue frying the remaining squid. Place on serving dishes and garnish each portion with lemon and parsley.

Imperial Asparagus

SERVES 2

This makes a lovely summer dish and is ideal for a special occasion as an appetizer or side dish.

PREPARATION: 15 mins
COOKING: 20 mins

1 pound asparagus
1½ tbsps butter or margarine
1½ tbsps all-purpose flour
⅔ cup chicken broth
5 tbsps dry white wine
1 egg yolk
2 tbsps heavy cream
Salt and white pepper
Pinch sugar, optional

1. Break off the woody ends of the asparagus then trim the spears to make them all the same length. Using a swivel vegetable peeler, pare the stalks up to the tips.

2. Tie the spears in a loose bundle and stand them upright in a deep saucepan of lightly salted boiling water. Alternatively, place the spears in a large skillet of boiling salted water and place the skillet half on and half off the heat, with the tips of the asparagus off the heat.

3. Cook, uncovered, for about 12-15 minutes, or until the asparagus is tender. Drain and keep the asparagus warm in a covered serving dish.

4. Melt the butter in a heavy-based saucepan. Remove from the heat and stir in the flour. Gradually beat in the broth and add the wine. Stir until the sauce is smooth and then place over a low heat.

5. Bring the sauce to the boil, stirring constantly, and allow to boil about 1-2 minutes, or until thickened.

6. Beat the egg yolk and cream together and add a few tablespoons of the hot sauce. Return the egg-and-cream mixture to the pan, stirring constantly. Reheat if necessary, but do not allow the sauce to boil. Add salt and white pepper and a pinch of sugar if wished. Pour sauce over asparagus and serve immediately.

Step 1 Hold the trimmed asparagus in your hand and remove the skin in thin strips, using a swivel vegetable peeler.

Creamy Dressed Dungeness Crab

SERVES 2

This makes a delicious warm weather salad for lunches, or light dinners.

PREPARATION: 45 mins
COOKING: 10 mins

---

2 medium Dungeness crabs, boiled
2 tbsps oil
4 green onions (scallions)
1 small green bell pepper, finely chopped
1 stick celery, finely chopped
1 clove garlic, crushed
¾ cup mayonnaise
1 tbsp mild mustard
Dash each Tabasco and Worcestershire sauce
1 piece canned pimiento or ortega chili, drained and finely chopped
2 tbsps minced parsley
Salt and pepper
Shredded lettuce

---

1. To shell the crabs, first remove all the legs and the large claws by twisting and pulling them away from the body. Turn the shell over and, using your thumbs, push the body away from the flat shell. Set the body aside.

2. Remove the stomach sack and the lungs or "dead man's fingers" and discard them. Using a small teaspoon, scrape the brown body meat out of the flat shell.

3. Using a sharp knife, cut the body of the crab in four pieces and use a skewer to push out all the meat.

4. Crack the large claws and remove the meat. Crack the legs and remove the meat from them. Discard the small, thin legs. Set all the meat aside. Scrub the shells if you intend to use them for serving.

5. Heat the oil in a small skillet. Chop the white parts of the green onions (scallions) and add to the oil with the green bell pepper, celery, and garlic. Sauté over a gentle heat for about 10 minutes, stirring often, to soften the vegetables but not brown them. Remove from the heat and set aside. When cool, add the mayonnaise, mustard, Tabasco, Worcestershire sauce, pimiento or ortega chili, and finely chopped tops of the green onions (scallions).

6. Spoon the reserved brown meat from the crabs back into each shell or arrange on a serving platter. Mix the remaining crabmeat with the dressing. Do not overmix the sauce, as the crabmeat should stay in large pieces. Spoon this over the brown meat, sprinkle with chopped parsley, and place the crab shells (if using) on serving dishes, surrounding them with shredded lettuce. Sprinkle with parsley and serve immediately.

Spanish Potato Omelet

SERVES 2

This makes a good lunch or supper dish, if served with salad and bread.

PREPARATION: 20 mins
COOKING: 30 mins

6 tbsps olive oil
2 cups potatoes, peeled and thinly sliced
Salt and pepper
1 medium onion, thinly sliced
4 large eggs
1 tomato, skinned, seeded, and sliced
1 green onion (scallion), chopped

1. Heat the oil in a large nonstick skillet and add the potatoes. Sprinkle lightly with salt and pepper and cook over medium heat until golden brown and crisp.

2. Add the onion once the potatoes begin to brown slightly. Turn the potatoes and onions over occasionally so that they brown evenly. They should take about 20 minutes to soften and brown.

3. Beat the eggs with a pinch of salt and pepper and pour the mixture over the vegetables in the pan. Allow the mixture to run underneath the vegetables. Cook over a gentle heat until the bottom browns lightly.

Step 3 Push the eggs and potatoes back from the sides of the pan using a fork.

Step 4 Slide pan under a preheated broiler to brown the top of the omelet.

4. Slide the pan under a preheated broiler to brown the top of the omelet and set the eggs. Garnish with the tomato and green onion (scallion) and serve in wedges.

15

Buttered Shrimp

SERVES 2

This makes an elegant entrée, yet it is surprisingly easy to make.

PREPARATION: 35 mins
COOKING: 20 mins

2 pounds cooked unpeeled shrimp
¼ cup butter, softened
Pinch each salt, white pepper, and cayenne pepper
1 clove garlic, crushed
6 tbsps fine dry breadcrumbs
2 tbsps minced parsley
4 tbsps sherry
Lemon wedges or slices, to garnish

1. To prepare the shrimp, remove the heads and legs first.

Step 1 Remove the heads and legs from the shrimp first. Remove any roe at this time.

Step 2 Pull off the tail shell and carefully remove the tip.

2. Peel off the shells, carefully removing the tail shells.

3. Use a cocktail stick to remove the black vein running down the length of the rounded side.

4. Arrange the shrimp in a shallow casserole or individual dishes.

5. Combine the remaining ingredients, except the lemon garnish, mixing well.

6. Spread the mixture over the shrimp, and place in an oven preheated to 375°F. Cook about 20 minutes, or until the butter melts and the crumbs become crisp. Garnish with lemon wedges or slices.

17

Sweet-Sour Fish

SERVES 2

In China, this dish is almost always prepared with freshwater fish, but sea bass is also an excellent choice. It is a spectacular dish for entertaining.

PREPARATION: 25 mins
COOKING: 15-20 mins

---

1 sea bass, gray mullet or catfish, weighing about 2 pounds, cleaned
1 tbsp dry sherry
Few slices fresh ginger
½ cup sugar
6 tbsps cider vinegar
1 tbsp soy sauce
2 tbsps cornstarch
1 clove garlic, crushed
2 green onions (scallions), shredded
1 small carrot, peeled and finely shredded
2 tbsps bamboo shoots, shredded

---

1. Rinse the fish well inside and out. Make three diagonal cuts on each side of the fish with a sharp knife.

2. Trim off the fins, apart from the dorsal fin on top. Trim the tail to two neat points.

3. Place the fish in a wok, add enough water to cover the fish, then remove the fish. Bring the water to the boil. Add the fish, with the sherry and ginger. Cover the wok tightly and remove

Step 2 Using kitchen scissors, trim off all the fins, except for the dorsal fin on top.

at once from the heat. Allow to stand 15-20 minutes to let the fish cook in the residual heat.

4. To test if the fish is cooked, pull the dorsal fin – if it comes away easily the fish is done. If not, return the wok to the heat and bring to the boil. Remove from the heat and leave the fish to stand a further 5 minutes. Transfer the fish to a heated serving platter and keep it warm. Remove all but 4 tbsps of the fish cooking liquid from the wok. Add the remaining ingredients including the vegetables and cook, stirring constantly, until the sauce thickens. Spoon some of the sauce over the fish to serve and serve the rest separately.

Tomato Beef Stir-Fry

SERVES 2

East meets West in a dish that is lightning-fast to cook and tastes like a "barbecue" sauced stir-fry.

PREPARATION: 25 mins, plus 4 hours marinating
COOKING: 20 mins

---

8 ounces sirloin or rump steak
1 clove garlic, crushed
3 tbsps wine vinegar
3 tbsps oil
Pinch each sugar, salt, and pepper
2 tsps ground cumin
½ small red bell pepper, sliced
½ small green bell pepper, sliced
½ cup baby corn
2 green onions (scallions), shredded
Oil for frying

Tomato Sauce
2 tbsps oil
½ medium onion, finely chopped
½-1 green chili, finely chopped
1 clove garlic, crushed
4 fresh ripe tomatoes, skinned, seeded and chopped
3 sprigs fresh coriander (cilantro)
2 tbsps tomato paste
1 bayleaf

---

1. Slice the meat thinly across the grain.

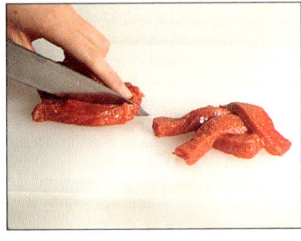

Step 1 Slice the meat thinly across the grain.

Combine in a plastic bag with the next 7 ingredients. Tie the bag and toss the ingredients inside to coat them. Place in a bowl and leave for about 4 hours.

2. Heat the oil for the sauce and cook the onion, chili, and garlic to soften but not brown. Add the remaining sauce ingredients and cook for about 15 minutes over a gentle heat. Purée in a food processor until smooth.

3. Heat a large skillet and add the meat, discarding the marinade. Cook to brown and set aside. Add about 1 tbsp of oil and cook the peppers for about 2 minutes. Add the corn and onions and return the meat to the pan. Cook for a further 1 minute and add the sauce. Cook to heat through and serve immediately.

Veal with Peaches and Pine Nuts

SERVES 2

This dish is quite expensive, but very easy and quick to prepare and cook. Pork fillet or chicken breast will taste equally good in this sauce.

PREPARATION: 15 mins
COOKING: 20 mins

---

2 small ripe peaches
3 tbsps brandy or sherry
4 small, thin veal scallops
Salt and pepper
2 tbsps oil
⅔ cup dry white wine
Pinch of cinnamon
1 small bayleaf
2 tsps cornstarch mixed with 1 tbsp water
Pinch sugar (optional)
2 tbsps pine nuts, toasted

---

1. Skin the peaches by dropping them into boiling water for about 30 seconds. Remove immediately to a bowl of cold water and leave to cool completely. Use a small, sharp knife to remove the skins.

2. Cut the peaches in half, pit them, and place the peaches in a deep bowl with the brandy or sherry. Stir the peach halves to coat them completely.

3. Heat the oil in a skillet and fry the scallops on both sides until golden brown. Pour the wine over them and add the cinnamon, bayleaf, salt and pepper, and cover the pan. Cook over a low heat 10-15 minutes or until the veal is tender and cooked through.

4. When the veal is cooked, remove it to a serving platter and keep it warm. Add the cornstarch mixture to the pan and bring to the boil. Cook until thickened and cleared.

5. Remove the peaches from the brandy and slice them. Add the peaches and the brandy to the thickened sauce mixture and bring to the boil. Allow to cook rapidly about 1 minute. Add the sugar, if using. Spoon the peaches and sauce over the veal scallops and sprinkle with the toasted pine nuts. Serve immediately.

Step 1 Place peaches in boiling water for 30 seconds.

Gingered Pork Chops

SERVES 2

Ginger-flavored cookies give a spicy lift to pork chop gravy, thickening it at the same time.

PREPARATION: 20 mins
COOKING: 50 mins

2 even-sized pork loin or shoulder chops
½ tsp ground black pepper
Pinch salt
½ tsp ground ginger
Good pinch each rubbed sage, ground coriander (cilantro), and paprika
2 tbsps oil
½ small onion, finely chopped
½ stick celery, finely chopped
1 clove garlic, crushed
1 cup chicken broth
6-7 ginger cookies, crushed

1. Trim the chops of any excess fat. Mix together the seasoning, herbs, and spices, and press the mixture firmly onto both sides of the chops.

2. Heat half the oil in a large skillet and, when hot, add the chops. Brown on both sides and remove to a plate.

3. Heat the remaining oil in the pan and add the onion, celery, and garlic. Cook until soft, then add the broth.

4. Return the chops to the pan, cover and cook about 30-40 minutes, or until tender.

5. When the chops are cooked, remove them to a serving dish and keep them warm. Stir the crushed cookies into the pan liquid and bring it to the boil.

6. Stir constantly to allow the cookies to soften and thicken the liquid. Boil rapidly for about 3 minutes to reduce, then pour the sauce over the chops to serve.

Step 5 Use the crushed ginger cookies to thicken the pan liquid. Cook slowly until dissolved.

Spiced Lamb

SERVES 2

Tender sautéed lamb is delicious in a sauce fragrant with herbs and spices.

Preparation: 25 mins, plus 4 hours marinating
Cooking: 25 mins

---

12 ounces lamb neck fillet
½ tsp fresh dill, chopped
½ tsp rosemary, crushed
½ tsp fresh thyme, chopped
1 tsp mustard seeds, slightly crushed
1 bayleaf
½ tsp coarsely ground black pepper
¼ tsp ground allspice
Juice 1 lemon
⅔ cup red wine
1 tbsp oil
½ small red bell pepper, sliced
½ cup button mushrooms, left whole
1 tbsp butter
1½ tbsps all-purpose flour
⅓ cup beef broth
Salt

---

1. Place the lamb in a shallow dish and sprinkle with the dill, rosemary, thyme, and mustard seeds. Add the bayleaf, pepper, allspice, lemon juice, and wine, and stir to coat the meat thoroughly with the marinade. Refrigerate 4 hours.

2. Heat the oil in a skillet and add the red bell pepper and mushrooms. Cook until the vegetables are softened. Remove with a slotted spoon.

3. Reheat the oil in the pan and add the lamb fillet, well drained and patted dry. Reserve the marinade. Brown the meat quickly on all sides to seal. Remove from the skillet and set aside with the vegetables.

4. Melt the butter in the skillet and when foaming add the flour. Lower the heat and cook the flour slowly until brown. Pour in the beef broth and the marinade. Bring to the boil and return the vegetables and lamb to the pan. Cook about 10-12 minutes, or until the lamb is tender, but still pink inside.

5. Slice the lamb fillet thinly on the diagonal and arrange on plates. Remove the bayleaf from the sauce and spoon the sauce over the meat.

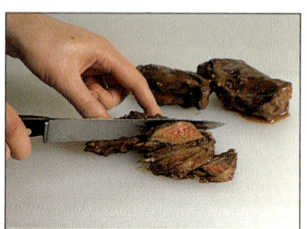

Step 5 To serve, slice the lamb on the diagonal, using a large sharp carving knife.

Rock Cornish Hens with Juniper Sauce

SERVES 2
This sauce will work equally well with quail, or with wild game.

PREPARATION: 30 mins
COOKING: 45 mins

2 Rock Cornish Hens
½ cup chicken liver pâté
1 tbsp brandy
6 slices streaky bacon
4 tbsps smoked bacon, chopped
1 onion, finely chopped
½ carrot, finely chopped
1 stick celery, finely chopped
1 tbsp juniper berries
2 tbsps all-purpose flour
1¼ cups broth
⅔ cup dry white wine
1 tsp tomato paste (optional)
Salt and pepper

1. Pluck any pin feathers from the birds with tweezers or singe them over a gas flame.

2. Mix the pâté and brandy together and spread on the insides of each bird.

3. Tie the bacon on the birds to cover the breasts and roast them in an oven preheated to 400°F, for 35-40 minutes.

4. Meanwhile, place the chopped bacon in a heavy-based saucepan over low heat. Cook slowly to render the fat.

5. Add the vegetables and juniper berries, and cook until the vegetables begin to brown lightly.

6. Add the flour and cook until golden-brown.

7. Add the broth gradually, stirring continuously. Bring to the boil then simmer, partially covered, for 20-25 minutes. Add more broth or water as necessary.

8. Skim the fat from the roasting pan and discard it. Add pan juices to the sauce and pour in the juices from the cavity of each bird.

9. Strain the sauce into a clean pan and add the wine and tomato paste, if using.

10. Bring to the boil for about 3 minutes to reduce slightly. Season with salt and pepper and serve with the hens.

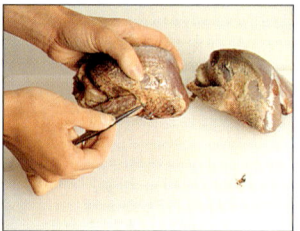

Step 1 Remove pin feathers with tweezers or singe the birds over an open flame.

Filled Beef Rolls

SERVES 2

This recipe is a Polish version of beef olives.

PREPARATION: 20 mins
COOKING: 45 mins

4 thin frying steaks, trimmed of fat
About 4 tbsps mustard
1 dill pickle, cut into thin strips
4 tbsps cooked ham steak, cut into thin strips
1 green onion (scallion), shredded
2 tbsps oil
1 tbsp all-purpose flour
⅔ cup beef broth
2 tbsps white wine
2 tsps tomato paste
Salt and pepper
2 tbsps sour cream or thick yogurt
Minced parsley

1. Place each steak between two sheets of damp parchment paper and flatten with a steak hammer or rolling pin.

2. Spread the meat thinly with some mustard and divide the dill pickle, ham and onion among all the slices.

3. Fold about ½ inch of the meat from each side toward the center. Roll the meat around the filling as for a burito and secure with cocktail sticks or tie with fine string.

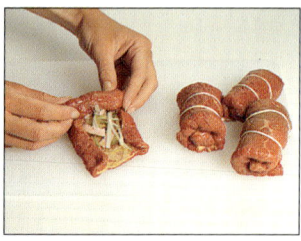

Step 3 Roll the ends of the meat over the filling to cover completely and secure with string or cocktail sticks.

4. Heat the oil in a large skillet and when hot, brown the beef rolls. Remove the meat and set aside.

5. Add the flour to the pan and allow to cook until light brown. Gradually stir in the stock and add the wine, tomato paste, salt, and pepper. Bring to the boil then simmer for 1 minute.

6. Return the beef rolls to the pan and spoon some of the sauce over them. Cover and cook over a low heat for 25-30 minutes. Add more liquid as necessary during cooking.

7. When the beef rolls are cooked, transfer them to a serving dish and remove the cocktail sticks or string. Spoon the sauce over them, and top with the sour cream and minced parsley.

Pork Fillet with Prunes

SERVES 2

This rich dish with its creamy sauce and wine-soaked prunes originates from the Loire region of France.

PREPARATION: 25 mins plus soaking time
COOKING: 15 mins

1 cup pitted no-soak prunes
1 cup white wine
1 small pork fillet
Seasoned flour to coat
2 tbsps butter or margarine
1½ tsps cranberry jelly
½ cup heavy cream
Minced parsley to garnish

1. Marinate the prunes in the white wine 20 minutes.

2. Slice the pork fillet on the diagonal into 1-inch thick pieces. Flatten them slightly with the palm of the hand and dredge them with seasoned flour. Melt the butter in a heavy-based skillet. When it is foaming, add the pork and cook until lightly browned on both sides.

3. Add half the soaking liquid from the prunes, cover the pan, and cook very gently over a moderate heat about 15 minutes, adding more of the wine if necessary.

4. When the pork is tender, pour the liquid into a small saucepan and bring to the boil. Reduce by about a fourth and add the cranberry jelly. Stir until dissolved and then add the cream. Bring the sauce back to the boil and boil rapidly until the sauce is reduced and thickened slightly. Pour the sauce over the meat, add the prunes and reheat. Transfer to a serving dish and sprinkle with a little minced parsley.

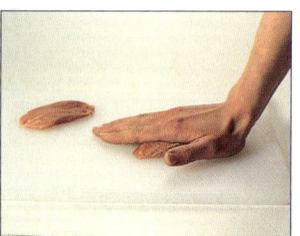

Step 2 Slice the pork fillet and flatten the slices with the palm of the hand.

Step 4 Whisk the cranberry jelly into the boiling sauce.

Garnished Pepper Steaks

SERVES 2
Serve with rice, pasta or new potatoes.

Preparation: 20 mins
Cooking: 15-20 mins

---

2 sirloin or rump steaks about 4 ounces each in weight
1 clove garlic, crushed
Salt and freshly ground black pepper
Oil

Sauce
1 shallot, finely chopped
2 tbsps small capers
¼ cup sliced mushrooms
1 tbsp flour
⅔ cup beef broth
2 tsps mild mustard
1 tsp Worcestershire sauce
4 tbsps white wine
1 tsp lemon juice
Pinch each of thyme and rosemary

Garnish
4 baby cobs of sweetcorn, cut in half
½ each small green and red bell pepper, thinly sliced
2 fresh pimientos, stem and seeds removed and cut in half
2 ripe tomatoes, skinned, seeded and cut into thin strips

Step 1 Press the steaks firmly against the base of the pan using a metal spatula.

1. Rub the crushed garlic, salt, and pepper into both sides of each steak. Heat a large skillet and brush the surface lightly with oil. Place the steaks in the hot pan and press them down firmly with a metal spatula to seal. Turn over and repeat. Remove the steaks to a plate and add 1 tbsp of oil to the pan.

2. Add the shallot, capers, and mushrooms and cook about 1 minute. Sprinkle with the flour and cook to brown lightly. Add the broth and stir well. Add the remaining sauce ingredients and bring to the boil.

3. Add the corn cobs and peppers to the sauce and return the steaks to the pan. Cook 6-8 minutes or until the steaks are cooked to taste. Add the remaining ingredients to the sauce. Transfer the steaks to a heated serving platter, and spoon the sauce over them.

Duck in Caper Sauce

SERVES 2

A sweet-and-sour sauce with the tang of capers is a perfect accompaniment to a rich meat such as duck.

PREPARATION: 20 mins, plus 1-2 hours standing
COOKING: 1½ hours

---

1 × 4-pound duck
1 clove garlic, crushed
Salt and pepper
1 tbsp oil
3 tbsps butter or margarine
1¼ cups chicken broth
⅔ cup water
4 tbsps sugar
1 tbsp vinegar or lemon juice
4 tsps cornstarch mixed with 2 tbsps water
6 tbsps capers

---

1. Rub the cavity of the duck with the crushed garlic and sprinkle with salt and pepper. Leave to stand in a cool place 1-2 hours, but do not refrigerate.

2. Heat the oil in a heavy skillet or roasting pan and when hot add the butter or margarine. Prick the duck skin all over with a sharp fork then brown on all sides in the hot fat. Transfer the duck to a saucepan or flameproof casserole.

3. Pour the broth over the duck, cover, and simmer over medium heat about 1½ hours, or until the duck is tender.

4. Meanwhile, heat the water and sugar together slowly in a small, heavy-based saucepan until the sugar dissolves.

5. Once the sugar is dissolved, increase the heat and boil rapidly until it caramelizes. Remove from the heat and slowly add in the vinegar or lemon juice. It will splutter so avoid any splashes. Add several tablespoons of the cooking liquid from the duck and set the caramel over a medium heat. Allow the mixture to come to the boil, stirring constantly.

6. When the duck is tender, remove it to a heated serving dish. Skim off the fat from the cooking liquid and discard. Add several tablespoons of the duck cooking liquid to the cornstarch mixture. Return this to the rest of the liquid and bring to the boil. Add the capers and stir over a high heat until the sauce clears and thickens. Add the caramel and stir until the sauce is thick.

7. Slice the duck into portions or serve whole and spoon some of the sauce over it. Serve the rest of the sauce separately.

Brown Bread Crumble

SERVES 2

The unusual crumble topping on this dessert is simple to make, high in fiber, and very tasty.
Serve with custard sauce or pouring cream for special occasions

PREPARATION: 15 mins
COOKING: 20 mins

---

1 cup tart apples, cored and sliced
½ cup raspberries
4 tbsps fresh wholewheat breadcrumbs
4 tbsps raw oatmeal
1½ tbsps light muscovado sugar
½ tsp ground cinnamon
¼ tsp ground cardamom
3 tbsps butter or margarine

---

1. Arrange the apple slices in a small pie pan and scatter the raspberries over the top.

2. Put the breadcrumbs, oatmeal, sugar, and spices in a large bowl. Mix together well to distribute the spices evenly.

3. Add the butter and rub into the mixture until well mixed.

4. Spoon the topping over the prepared fruits and smooth the top with a spoon.

5. Bake in an oven preheated to 375°F, for 20-25 minutes or until the topping is lightly browned and the filling piping hot.

Blueberry Snow with Mint

SERVES 2

This simple dessert, which is quick and easy to make, should be eaten the same day it is prepared.

PREPARATION: 15 mins

½ cup fresh or frozen blueberries
3 tbsps sugar
1 egg white
⅓ cup whipping cream
⅓ cup plain yogurt
1 tbsp chopped fresh mint

Garnish
Whole sprigs fresh mint
Finger cookies or vanilla wafers

1. Combine the blueberries and 1 tbsp of the sugar in a small, heavy-based pan. Cook slowly until juice forms and the blueberries soften. Set aside to cool completely.

2. When the blueberries are cool, whisk the egg white until stiff but not dry.

3. Gradually whisk in the remaining sugar. Whisk well in between each addition of sugar, until stiff peaks form and the egg white is smooth and glossy.

4. Whip the cream until thick, and combine with the yogurt.

5. Fold the egg white into the cream-and-yogurt mixture, along with the cooled blueberries and the chopped mint. Do not over-fold, the mixture should look marbled.

6. Spoon into individual serving dishes and garnish with the whole sprigs of mint. Serve in tall sundae glasses with finger cookies or vanilla wafers.

Cherry Compôte

SERVES 2

This makes a special, elegant dessert, but an easy one, too. The contrast of hot brandied cherries and cold ice cream or whipped cream is sensational.

PREPARATION: 10 mins
COOKING: 10 mins

1½ cups canned black, pitted cherries, juice reserved
1-2 tbsps sugar
2 tbsps brandy
Vanilla ice cream or whipped cream, to serve

1. Combine the cherry juice with the sugar and heat through to dissolve it. Add the cherries to the juice.

2. Pour the brandy into a separate saucepan. Heat the brandy and ignite with a match. Combine the brandy with the fruit and leave

Step 2 Add the flaming brandy to the cherries and leave until the flames die down naturally.

until the flames die down naturally.

3. Serve the fruit over ice cream or spoon into serving dishes and top with whipped cream. Serve immediately.

Index

Appetizers:
    Fried Squid 8
    Imperial Asparagus 10
Blueberry Snow with Mint 40
Brown Bread Crumble 38
Buttered Shrimp 16
Cherry Compôte 42
Creamy Dressed Dungeness Crab 12
Desserts:
    Blueberry Snow with Mint 40
    Brown Bread Crumble 38
    Cherry Compôte 42
Duck in Caper Sauce 36
Filled Beef Rolls 30
Fried Squid 8
Garnished Pepper Steaks 34
Gingered Pork Chops 24
Imperial Asparagus 10
Lunches and Suppers:
    Buttered Shrimp 16
    Creamy Dressed Dungeness Crab 12

    Spanish Potato Omelet 14
    Tomato Beef Stir-Fry 20
Main Courses:
    Duck in Caper Sauce 36
    Filled Beef Rolls 30
    Garnished Pepper Steaks 34
    Gingered Pork Chops 24
    Pork Fillet with Prunes 32
    Rock Cornish Hens with Juniper
        Sauce 28
    Spiced Lamb 26
    Sweet-Sour Fish 18
    Veal with Peaches and Pine Nuts 22
Pork Fillet with Prunes 32
Rock Cornish Hens with Juniper
    Sauce 28
Spanish Potato Omelet 14
Spiced Lamb 26
Sweet-Sour Fish 18
Tomato Beef Stir-Fry 20
Veal with Peaches and Pine Nuts 22